A British Teatime Recipe Book

Twelve Teatime recipes and watercolor photos included, plus thirteen styled blank pages to include your own recipes, History of British Teatime, How to Host a British Tea Party, twelve beautiful watercolor vintage art pages, and more!

Teresa Davis

A British Teatime Recipe Book
Copyright (© 2023) Teresa Davis - All rights reserved

Cover Design by Teresa Davis

No part of this book may be reproduced or transmitted in any form or by any means, electronic or mechanical, including photocopy, recording, or any information storage or retrieval system, without the prior written consent form from the author, except for non-commercial personal use as specifically granted by the author.

Under no circumstances will any blame or legal responsibility be held against the publisher, or author, for any damages, reparation, or monetary loss due to the information contained within this book, either directly or indirectly. You are responsible for your own choices, actions, and results.

This Recipe Book Belongs to: _____

Table of Contents

The History of the British Teatime Tradition ---------pgs. 5-6
How To Host a British Afternoon Tea Party ---------pg. 9
How To Host a British Tea Part for Children ---------pg. 10

Watercolor Art Pages:
Lady Adeline ---------pg. 7
Children Having a Glorious Tea Party ---------pg. 11
Afternoon Tea Party ---------pg.13
Afternoon Stroll in The Garden ---------pg. 21
Country Manor ---------pg. 29
Lady Katherine & Lord Derrick ---------pg. 33
Stately Manor ---------pg. 39
Two Sisters Having Tea ---------pg. 47
William Lucas---------pg. 63
Lady Caroline ---------pg. 65
Teapot ---------pg. 67
Lord Henry Davenport ---------pg. 69

Recipes:
1. Scones ---------pgs. 15-16
2. Victoria Sponge Cake ---------pgs. 17-18
3. Butter Shortbread Biscuits ---------pgs. 19-20
4. Ginger Biscuits also called Ginger Snaps ---------pgs. 23-24
5. Cucumber and Cream Cheese Sandwiches ---------pgs. 25-26
6. Egg Finger Sandwiches ---------pgs. 27-28
7. Mini Gugulhupf Cakes with Cream Cheese---------pgs. 31-32
8. Cherry, Pistachio and Marzipan Cake ---------pgs. 35-36
9. Roast Beef Sandwiches ---------pgs. 37-38
10. Truffled Deviled Eggs ---------pgs. 41-42
11. Sheet Pan Petit Fours ---------pgs. 43-44
12. Classic Cheese Scones---------pgs. 45-46
13. Styled Blank Recipe Pages (colored) ---------pgs. 49-62

British Teatime: A History and Why It's So Important to British People:

Tea has been a beloved beverage in Britain for over 350 years and has become an integral part of British culture. British teatime has become so crucial to the British people that it is considered a national institution. The history of teatime in Britain can be traced back to the 17th century when tea first arrived in England from China. Initially, it was considered a luxury item and was only consumed by the wealthy. However, by the 18th century, tea had become more affordable and became a popular beverage among all classes of society.

Teatime became a formal ritual during the Victorian era when the Duchess of Bedford popularized the idea of afternoon tea. In the mid-19th century, people typically ate just two meals daily, breakfast and dinner, served quite late in the evening. The Duchess of Bedford, known to become hungry around 4 p.m., started taking a light meal of tea, sandwiches, and cakes to tide her over until dinner. She soon began inviting friends to join her, and this social event became known as afternoon tea or high tea. Teatime quickly became a staple of British culture, and it's now a much-cherished tradition passed down from generation to generation. Classic afternoon tea is still enjoyed in Britain, with a pot of tea, scones, clotted cream, and jam.

The Three Types of Teatimes:

Elevenses, Afternoon Tea, and High Tea are different meals or snacks traditionally taken at specific times of the day.
1. *Elevenses*: This is a mid-morning snack that is usually taken around 11 am and typically consists of tea or coffee and a light snack such as a scone, muffin, or biscuit.
2. *Afternoon Tea*: This meal is more substantial than Elevenses and is typically taken between 3 pm and 5 pm. It traditionally consists of tea, sandwiches, scones, and cakes or pastries.
3. *High Tea*: This is the most substantial of the three and usually takes between 5 pm and 7 pm. It is also known as "meat tea" and traditionally includes hot dishes such as meat pies, casseroles, sausages, bread and butter, cakes, and tea.

It's worth noting that the terms "Afternoon Tea" and "High Tea" are often used interchangeably outside of Britain, but they are distinct in British culture. Afternoon Tea is more formal and elegant, with High Tea being more of a working-class meal.

So, why is teatime so crucial to the British people?

Firstly, it provides a break in the day, a chance to sit down and relax with a cup of tea and some delicious treats. It's an opportunity to catch up with friends and family, and it's also a chance to take a break from work and recharge.

Secondly, teatime is an integral part of British social culture. It's a way of connecting with others and is often the centerpiece of social gatherings such as weddings, birthdays, and other celebrations. Teatime is a time to come together, share stories, and enjoy each other's company.

Remember, sandwiches are the core savory course, which you start with, if you are having a core substantial afternoon tea.

In conclusion, British teatime is an essential part of British culture that has stood the test of time. It has become an institution representing British hospitality, warmth, and connection values, whether it's enjoyed in the comfort of one's own home or a fancy tearoom, a teatime tradition that continues to be cherished by the British people.

Lady Adeline

HOW TO HOST A BRITISH AFTERNOON TEA PARTY FOR ADULTS:

Afternoon tea is quintessentially a British tradition that dates back to the early 1800s. It's a sophisticated affair, perfect for celebrating special occasions or catching up with friends over a cuppa and some sweet treats. If you're looking to throw your own British afternoon tea party, here are some tips and ideas to get you started:

1. Set the scene: Create an elegant and traditional atmosphere with vintage tea sets, lace tablecloths, and fresh flowers. Set out tiered cake stands, serving plates, teacups, and saucers for an authentic look. Always remember, wear your fanciest clothing to a tea party.

2. Choose your teas: Offer a variety of black, green, and herbal teas to suit all tastes. Blends like Earl Grey and English Breakfast are always popular, but you could try something unusual like Darjeeling or a fruit tea.

3. Plan your menu: Alongside your teas, you'll want to serve a selection of sweet and savory treats. Finger sandwiches are a must – like cucumber and cream cheese, smoked salmon and cream cheese, or egg and cress. Scones with clotted cream and jam are another staple, as are cakes and pastries like Victoria Sponge, lemon drizzle, and mini quiches.

4. Don't forget the etiquette: Remind your guests to hold their teacups by the handle, not to stir their tea too vigorously, and to eat their sandwiches with their fingers, not a knife and fork. It's also customary to serve the tea before the food.

5. Add some entertainment: Consider playing background music or hiring a live musician to play classical or jazz tunes. Weather permitting, you could also set up a game of croquet or lawn bowls in the garden.

Following these tips, you can host a memorable and authentic British afternoon tea party that will transport your guests to the elegant days of old England. So put the kettle on and start planning your menu – it's time to start the party!

HOW TO HOST A BRITISH AFTERNOON TEA PARTY FOR CHILDREN:

Hosting a tea party for your child can be a fantastic way to create special memories and share in the charm of British culture. Here are some tips to make your child's tea party a success:

1.Set the scene: Create a tea party atmosphere by decorating your space with tea-themed decors, such as teacups, saucers, and floral arrangements.

2.Dress up: Encourage your child and guests to wear fancy clothes, hats, and gloves. This will add to the fun and make the event feel more special.

3.Plan the menu: Plan a menu that includes traditional British tea treats, such as scones, cakes, sandwiches, and biscuits. Make sure to offer a variety of tea options as well.

4.Teatime etiquette: Teach your child and guests about teatime etiquette, such as holding the teacup with two hands and using a small spoon for stirring.

5.Activities: Plan tea party activities, such as a hat decorating station or a teacup relay race, to keep the children entertained.

Follow these tips, and you can create a delightful British tea party experience that your child and guests will cherish for years.

Children Having a Glorious Tea Party

Afternoon Tea Party

Teatime Recipes

RECIPE	Scones		
YIELD	8	COOKTIME	10 mins

INGREDIENTS

8 oz plain flour
1 tsp bicarbonate of soda
2 tsp of cream of tartar
½ tsp salt
1 ½ oz butter
¼ pint milk-about

DIRECTIONS

Sieve the flour, salt bicarb, and cream of tartar into a bowl. Rub in the butter Until the mixture looks like fine breadcrumbs. Add enough milk to form a soft but not sticky dough. Use a round bladed knife to mix. Turn onto a floured surface and knead gently. Roll out the dough until about ½ inch thick and cut into rounds with a 2 in. pastry cutter. Place on a lightly-floured baking sheet, sprinkle with flour over scones and bake for 10 minutes until risen and golden.

NOTES

THE HISTORY OF SCONES

British scones are a beloved pastry enjoyed all around the world. These light, fluffy treats are often served with a generous dollop of clotted cream and strawberry jam and are an afternoon tea staple. But where did this tasty treat come from, and how did it become such a beloved part of British cuisine?

The history of scones can be traced back to Scotland in the early 16th century. The word "scone" is derived from the Old Scot's word "scone," which means "a shapeless mass or lump." The original scones were made with oats and baked on a griddle. They were often round, flat, and cut into triangular sections for serving.

As scones spread throughout the United Kingdom, the recipe began to evolve. In England, scones were often made with wheat flour instead of oats and baked in the oven instead of on a griddle. This led to a fluffier, lighter texture now characteristic of modern British scones.

Scones continued to gain popularity throughout the 19th and 20th centuries. They were often served at afternoon tea, a popular tradition in the mid-1800s. At this time, the upper classes would gather for tea and snacks in the late afternoon, a practice that soon spread throughout society.

Today, scones are a staple of British cuisine and are enjoyed worldwide. They can be served with various toppings, from clotted cream and jam to butter and honey. They're also a popular base for savory dishes, such as cheese and bacon scones.

In conclusion, British scones have a rich history that spans hundreds of years. From their humble origins as oat-based griddle cakes to their modern incarnation as fluffy, oven-baked treats, scones have been an essential part of British cuisine for centuries. So, the next time you enjoy a scone with a cup of tea, remember this beloved pastry's long and delicious history.

Teatime Recipes

RECIPE	Victorian Sponge Cake		
YIELD	1 7-inch round cake in 2 parts	COOKTIME	20-25 minutes 180 d. C.

INGREDIENTS

4 oz self rising flour
4 oz butter
4 oz caster sugar (fine granulated sugar)
2 large eggs, beaten
¼ tsp. vanilla essence

To finish cake: butter cream, or whipped cream, caster or icing sugar (confectioners' sugar) fruit or jam.

DIRECTIONS

Grease 2 6–7-inch round cake tins – line with greaseproof paper (greased). Sieve the flour. Cream the butter and sugar together with a wooden spoon until light and fluffy; gradually beat in the eggs and the vanilla essence, adding a spoonful of the sieved flour with the last amount. Carefully fold in the sieved flour.
Divide the mixture between the 2 sandwich tins.
Bake for 20-25 minutes until golden brown and the cake springs back when lightly pressed. Remove from oven and cool for a few minutes then turn out on a wire rack and leave until cold. Sandwich the cakes together with jam or jam and whipped cream, sprinkle with confectioners' sugar. For a strawberry or raspberry Victoria sponge, add sliced fruit to the whipped cream layer and add some on the top for decorations.

NOTES

THE HISTORY OF THE VICTORIAN SPONGE CAKE:

The Victorian Sponge Cake is a classic British dessert that has stood throughout the ages. This delicious cake, also known as it, is named after Queen Victoria, who reigned in the United Kingdom from 1837 to 1901. However, the history of this cake dates back to the mid-19th century when it was popularized in England.

During the Victorian time, there was a renewed interest in baking and cooking, and Victorian Sponge Cake became a staple of English cuisine. The cake was originally served as a light afternoon tea cake and quickly gained popularity among the middle and upper classes.

The cake's recipe's origin is unclear, but it appears to have been inspired by the French genoise cake. The French genoise cake is a similar sponge cake made with the same basic ingredients. However, the Victorian Sponge Cake has a softer texture and is easier to make, making it a more popular choice in England .Over the years, many variations of the Victorian Sponge Cake have been developed, including chocolate and fruit versions. However, the classic recipe remains the most popular and beloved.

Today, the Victorian Sponge Cake is still a favorite in British households and can be found in bakeries and tea shops across the country. It is often served at afternoon tea parties and special events in the United States.

In conclusion, the Victorian Sponge Cake is a classic British dessert with a rich history dating back to the mid-19th century. Its simple yet delicious recipe has made it a beloved treat for generations and continues to be a staple in English cuisine today. The Victorian Sponge Cake will satisfy any sweet tooth, whether enjoyed with a cup of tea or as a special dessert.

Teatime Recipes

RECIPE	Butter Shortbread Biscuits		
YIELD	8 pieces	COOKTIME	30-35 minutes

INGREDIENTS

4 oz plain flour
2 oz corn flour (cornstarch)
2 oz caster sugar (fine granulated sugar)
4 oz butter

You can add in extra ingredients to the basic recipe as modern tastes have changed:
Chocolate chips, nuts, cranberries, etc.

DIRECTIONS

Sieve together the flour and cornflour. Add sugar, rub in the butter, It is crumbly to begin but keep rubbing until it clings together in lumps. Turn onto a lightly dusted board or surface and knead lightly. Roll out to an 8-inch circle and place on a greased baking sheet. Mark out into 8 equal pieces and prick with a fork all over. Bake at 325 F for 30 to 36 minutes or until lightly golden brown. Leave on tray for 10 minutes to cool down and then lift with a wide fish slice and place carefully on a wire rack to cool.

NOTES

THE HISTORY OF THE BUTTER SHORTBREAD BISCUIT:

Butter shortbread biscuits have a rich history that dates back to medieval Scotland. The recipe evolved, and it became a luxury item for special occasions. Mary, Queen of Scots, was a notable fan of shortbread biscuits, and it's said that she loved the simple yet decadent treat so much that she even had a special recipe made with caraway seeds. Today, butter shortbread biscuits are enjoyed worldwide and remain a staple in many households. Their enduring appeal is due to the power of simple, wholesome ingredients, and their rich history reminds them of the importance of tradition and culture.

Making butter shortbread biscuits is a relatively simple process that involves just a few ingredients: butter, sugar, flour, and salt. The key to making perfect shortbread biscuits is to use high-quality ingredients and to handle the dough gently to avoid overworking it.

So why have butter shortbread biscuits remained so popular over the centuries? One reason is their versatility - butter shortbread biscuits can be enjoyed independently or used as a base for more complex desserts such as tarts and pies. But perhaps the main reason for their enduring appeal is their rich, buttery flavor and crumbly texture. Biting into a freshly baked shortbread biscuit and enjoying the rich, buttery goodness, nothing is better.

Butter shortbread biscuits are a beloved treat that has stood the test of time. From their humble origins in medieval Scotland to their modern-day popularity worldwide, they are a delicious reminder of the enduring appeal of simple, wholesome ingredients.

Afternoon Stroll in the Garden

Teatime Recipes

RECIPE	Ginger Snaps		
YIELD	24 or more	COOKTIME	20 minutes

INGREDIENTS

8 oz unsalted butter, softened
6 oz caster sugar (fine granulated sugar)
6 oz soft brown sugar
1 lard egg, beaten
12 oz all purpose flour
Pinch of salt
½ tsp baking powder
1 tsp grated nutmeg
1 TB ground ginger
1 tsp ground cloves
2 tsp ground cinnamon

Greaseproof paper can be substituted with wax paper. Caster sugar can be made by grinding regular sugar for a few seconds in a food processor.

DIRECTIONS

In a large baking bowl, cream the butter and sugars until light and creamy (use electric whisk if desired). Continue whisking as you slowly add the beaten egg a little bit at a time. Sift the dried ingredients together into another bowl.
Now stir in the flour mixture into the creamed butter mixture. It will turn into a soft dough. Place half the dough between 2 sheets of greaseproof paper and roll out to 1/8 – ¼-inch thick. Repeat with the other dough.
Now slide the dough onto baking sheets and put in the fridge for at least 2 hours. Heat oven to 350F/180C and grease a baking sheet with butter. Using a cookie cutter or a gingerbread man shape, cut out the biscuits. Place on the greased sheet and bake for 10 minutes.
Put the rest of the dough in the fridge while waiting for each batch to cook. Once removed from the oven, put on wire trays to cool and harden. Then they will have the perfect SNAP!

THE HISTORY OF THE GINGER BISCUITS ALSO CALLED GINER SNAPS:

Ginger biscuits, or ginger snaps, are a classic treat that pairs perfectly with British tea. These spiced cookies have a long history dating back to the Middle Ages when ginger was a highly prized and expensive ingredient. Originally, ginger biscuits were baked for medicinal purposes to help with digestive issues, but they became a popular snack over time. In the 19th century, ginger biscuits were mass-produced and became a staple in British households, especially during teatime.

During the Victorian era, ginger biscuits became a popular treat for high tea, a late-afternoon meal that often-included sandwiches, cakes, and tea. In addition, ginger biscuits were served on long voyages to combat seasickness. Ginger was often included in sailors' rations as ginger was believed to prevent nausea and indigestion.

Today, ginger biscuits remain a beloved snack in Britain. They can be found in almost every supermarket and bakery, and are often enjoyed with a cup of tea, which helps to balance out the spicy ginger flavor. Ginger biscuits also pair well with tea-time treats such as scones, clotted cream, and jam.

If you're looking to enjoy some ginger biscuits at home, many great recipes are available online that cater to different dietary needs. So, whether you prefer traditional ginger snaps or a more modern take on this classic cookie, there's a ginger biscuit recipe for everyone.

Teatime Recipes

RECIPE	Cucumber and Cream Cheese Sandwiches
YIELD	8 pieces

COOKTIME	

INGREDIENTS

English cucumber
Cream cheese
4 thin slices soft brown or white bread

DIRECTIONS

Slice the cucumbers very thing. Keep separate.

Spread cream cheese on 1 side of all the bread. Add the cucumber slices in neat rows so the sandwich remains flat, not lumpy. Put the 2nd slice over the first and cut off the crusts. Slice into triangles or squares with a cookie cutter into rounds.

The main rule with tea sandwiches is that the bread is thin and good quality and soft. The crust can be on or off as you like. Do not over fill the. They are meant to be easily eaten with you fingers in a few bites. Buttering the bread keeps the filling away from the bread and stops it from getting soggy. To keep the bread from drying out, cover with a damp tea towel/dish towel.

NOTES

There are many other flavors/flavours that can be used in the sandwich. Here are some favorites: Chicken and cranberry; shrimp and Marie Rose sauce; crab salad; ham and brie; cheddar cheese and pickles; and smoked salmon on pumpernickel bread.

THE HISTORY OF CUCUMBER AND CREAM CHEESE SANDWICHES:

Cucumber sandwiches have been a part of British tea culture for over a century. The combination of thinly sliced cucumbers and cream cheese spread on white bread became popular in the late 1800s when afternoon tea became a fashionable social event. The cucumber sandwich was considered a refreshing addition to the tea table, especially during the summer months. While the origin of the cucumber sandwich is unclear, it is believed to have been inspired by the Middle Eastern mezze dish of sliced cucumbers and yogurt. However, the addition of cream cheese is a distinctly British twist.

In the early 1900s, the cucumber sandwich became a staple of the traditional English afternoon tea, often served alongside other tea-time favorites such as scones and cakes. It was also a popular choice for women's gatherings such as garden parties and charity events.

Today, cucumber and cream cheese sandwiches remain a popular tea-time snack and can be found on the menu at many tea rooms and hotels throughout the UK.

Teatime Recipes

RECIPE	Egg Finger Sandwiches		
YIELD	8 small sandwiches	COOKTIME	8 mins. For the eggs

INGREDIENTS

4 slices soft white bread
4 eggs, hardboiled and peeled
Chives – 1 Tb chopped finely
White pepper
Malt vinegar
Homemade mayonnaise
1 egg yolk
Vegetable or groundnut oil
1 tsp white wine vinegar
½ tsp mustard powder
salt

DIRECTIONS

Boil the eggs and make the mayonnaise first.
Put the egg yolks in a bowl and whisk together and whisk in the mustard powder. Begin adding the oil, a few drops at a time, whisking as you do so. As it thickens, you can add the oil in a steady stream. Add the white wine vinegar and season with salt. Peel the eggs, and mash them with a fork. Mix in 2 Tb of the mayo and the chives, then season with salt and white pepper. Add a teaspoon of vinegar to start with, adding more if you think it's needed. Spread the mixture onto one slice of bread, top with the other, and cut into preferred sandwich shape. You can make squares, fingers, or triangles.

NOTES

THE HISTORY OF THE EGG FINGER SANDWICHES:

The egg finger sandwich has been quintessential in British teatime for centuries. The history of this delicious snack can be traced back to high tea early 18th century when it became a popular social event in England.

Initially, egg sandwiches were a simple and practical snack made with boiled eggs and bread. However, the recipe evolved over time, and new ingredients, such as mayonnaise and seasonings, were added to create a more flavorful and satisfying snack.

Today, egg finger sandwiches are a staple of British teatime and are often served alongside other classic snacks such as scones, cucumber sandwiches, and pastries. Whether enjoyed with tea or coffee, the egg finger sandwich remains a beloved part of British culinary tradition and a delicious and satisfying snack for any occasion.

Country Manor

Teatime Recipes

RECIPE	Mini Gugulhupf Cakes with Cream Cheese		
YIELD	6	COOKTIME	40 mins.

INGREDIENTS

- 1 1/3 cups (200g) plain flour
- 1/2 teaspoon baking powder
- 1/4 teaspoon bicarbonate of soda
- 1/4 teaspoon ground nutmeg
- 2 cups (440g) caster sugar
- 2 eggs
- 1/4 cup (60ml) rum
- 1/4 cup (60ml) milk
- 1/4 cup (60ml) sunflower oil
- 1 teaspoon vanilla extract
- 1 teaspoon ground cinnamon
- Strawberry jam, to serve

DIRECTIONS

1. Preheat the oven to 180°C. Grease and lightly flour six 1-cup (250ml) mini guglhupf molds. Sift the flour, baking powder, bicarbonate of soda and nutmeg into a large bowl, then stir in 1 cup (220g) sugar. Place the eggs, rum, milk, oil and vanilla in a separate large bowl and whisk to combine. Gradually add flour mixture and stir to combine. Divide batter among the molds and bake for 35-40 minutes until cakes are risen and pale golden.

2. Combine the cinnamon and remaining 1 cup (220g) sugar in a shallow dish. Cool the gugelhupf cakes slightly in molds, then invert and toss in the cinnamon sugar while still warm. Serve warm with jam to spread over.

NOTES

THE HISTORY OF THE MINI GUGULHUPF CAKES WITH CREAM CHEESE:

In recent years, mini Gugulhupf cakes with cream cheese have become a popular addition to British teatime menus. These delicious small cakes have a rich history, originating in Austria, where they were traditionally served at weddings and celebrations.

Traditionally, Gugulhupf cakes were made using a yeast-based batter, but many variations of the recipe have emerged over time. Some recipes use baking powder instead of yeast, while others incorporate ingredients like raisins or nuts to add flavor and texture.

The Gugulhupf cake gained popularity throughout Europe, and in the 19th century, it became a popular snack in Britain. However, when the addition of cream cheese filling was added, the mini Gugulhupf cake was on British teatime menus. Cream cheese filling has become a popular addition when it comes to serving mini Gugulhupf cakes. Adding a rich, creamy texture to the cakes perfectly complements their sweet, delicate flavor.

In recent years, mini Gugulhupf cakes with cream cheese have become a popular addition to British teatime menus. Many tea rooms and cafes now offer these delicious cakes as part of their afternoon tea service, alongside other classic snacks like scones, cucumber sandwiches, and pastries.

Overall, mini Gugulhupf cakes with cream cheese are a delightful and unique addition to any teatime menu and an excellent way to enjoy a sweet treat with tea or coffee.

Lady Kathrine and Lord Derrick

Teatime Recipes

RECIPE	Cherry, Pistachio and Marzipan Cake		
YIELD		COOKTIME	1 hr., 20 mins.

INGREDIENTS

- 300g cherries, pitted, finely chopped
- 150g marzipan, chopped into 1cm pieces
- 1 cup (150g) self-raising flour, sifted, plus 1 tbs extra
- 225g unsalted butter, softened
- 185g caster sugar
- Finely grated zest of 1 lemon
- 1 tsp orange blossom water
- 4 eggs
- 100g almond meal
- 1 tsp baking powder
- 1/3 cup (50g) unsalted pistachio kernels, lightly toasted, chopped
- Icing sugar, to dust

DIRECTIONS

1. Preheat the oven to 170°C. Grease and line a 20cm springform cake pan with baking paper, then wrap the outside with foil (this will prevent batter from leaking).
2. Toss cherries and marzipan in extra 1 tbs flour (this will help prevent them sinking), shake off excess and set aside.
3. In a large bowl, beat the butter, caster sugar and lemon zest with electric beaters for 3-5 minutes until thick and pale, then beat in orange blossom water.
4. Add the eggs, 1 at a time, beating well after each addition. Fold in flour, almond meal, baking powder and a pinch of salt, then stir through half the marzipan and cherries. Spread mixture into pan, sprinkle over remaining marzipan and cherries, then gently press into the batter, making sure they're just covered.
5. Bake for 20 minutes, then reduce oven to 160ºC and bake for a further 50-60 minutes until light golden and cooked through (cover loosely with foil if cake is browning too quickly).
6. Meanwhile, for the syrup. Place all the ingredients in a saucepan over low heat, then cook, stirring, for 1-2 minutes until sugar has dissolved. Increase heat to medium and cook for a further 1-2 minutes until thick and syrupy..
7. Pierce cake all over with a skewer, then drizzle over warm syrup. Sprinkle with pistachios and dust with icing sugar. Cool slightly, then remove cake from the pan and cool completely before serving.

THE HISTORY OF THE MINI GUGULHUPF CAKES WITH CREAM CHEESE:

Cherry, pistachio, and marzipan cake is a delectable dessert that has recently gained popularity in British teatime menus. The history of this cake dates back to the Middle Ages when dried fruits, nuts, and marzipan were commonly used in European desserts.

Over time, the recipe evolved, and fresh cherries and pistachios added a new dimension of flavor and texture to the classic marzipan cake. The cake is typically made using a marzipan base, then topped with fresh cherries and pistachios and baked to perfection.

Cherry, pistachio, and marzipan cake have become a beloved dessert among tea lovers in Britain and are often served at afternoon tea or other special occasions. Combining sweet cherries, nutty pistachios, and rich marzipan makes a delicious and satisfying dessert.

Recently, many tea rooms and cafes have started offering cherry, pistachio, and marzipan cake as part of their teatime menus, alongside other classic treats like scones, sandwiches, and pastries. Whether enjoyed with tea or coffee, this delightful dessert will satisfy any sweet tooth.

Teatime Recipes

RECIPE	Roast Beef Sandwiches		
YIELD	3-4 thin fingers or 4 triangles	COOKTIME	

INGREDIENTS

2 slices white sandwich bread or other kind, to taste
2 slices roast beef or more depending on size
1 tsp. mustard (wholegrain or Dijon)
1 tsp. butter

DIRECTIONS

1. Spread one slice of bread with butter and the other with a thin layer of mustard (if you like, you can also butter it underneath as well.)
2. Make a layer of roast beef on top of one of the slices of bread, going right to the edges and without gaps.
3. Top with the other slice of bread, trim off the crusts keeping the edges parallel as you do so.
4. Cut into either 3-4 thing fingers or four triangles.

NOTES

THE HISTORY OF THE ROAST BEEF SANDWICHES AND BRITISH TEATIME:

Roast beef sandwiches and British teatime traditions have a rich and fascinating history. Returning to the 18th century, roast beef became a staple of British cuisine and was often served as the centerpiece of Sunday dinners.

In the mid-19th century, the Earl of Sandwich famously popularized placing meat between two slices of bread, giving rise to the classic roast beef sandwich. Teatime, a British tradition dating back to the 17th century, was originally a light meal between lunch and dinner. As the custom grew popular, teatime evolved to include sandwiches, scones, cakes, and other sweet and savory treats.

Today, roast beef sandwiches and teatime continue to be beloved British culinary traditions that are enjoyed by people all over the world.

Stately Manor

Teatime Recipes

RECIPE	Truffled Deviled Eggs		
YIELD	24 Eggs	COOKTIME	Prep 14 min. Cook 13 mins.

INGREDIENTS

12 large eggs
1 cup mayonnaise
2 Tb finely chopped black truffle peelings
1 Tb truffle oil
Pinch of cayenne pepper
Chopped fresh chives, for garnish

DIRECTIONS

1. Put the eggs in a large pot and add enough water to cover by about 1 inch. Bring the pot to boil, cover and then turn off the heat and let sit for 13 minutes EXACTLY!
2. Drain the eggs and run them under cold water until cool; if you're not using them right away, put them in the fridge.
3. Peel the eggs and cut them in half lengthwise. Remove the yolks. Put the yolks in a small bowl and mash them with a fork. Add the mayonnaise, truffle peeling, truffle oil, and cayenne and whip until very light and fluffy.
4. Use a disposable pastry bag (or just buy zip top bags, fill them and cut off one corner – a very low-tech solution) to pipe the yolk mixture into the whites (or just spoon it in). Sprinkle with the chives to serve

THE HISTORY OF THE DEVILED EGGS:

Deviled eggs, also known as stuffed eggs or angel eggs, are a popular appetizer in American cuisine. The origin of stuffed eggs can be traced back to ancient Rome, where boiled eggs were seasoned with spices and served as an appetizer. The term "deviled" first appeared in the 18th century, when it was used to describe spicy or zesty foods. By the 19th century, deviled eggs had become a typical dish in America, often served at picnics, potlucks, and parties. Deviled eggs are typically made by slicing hard-boiled eggs in half, removing the yolks, and mixing them with mayonnaise, mustard, and other seasonings before returning the mixture to the egg whites. They are then often garnished with paprika, parsley, or other herbs.

As for whether deviled eggs are served at British afternoon teatime, they are not typically part of the traditional menu. Afternoon tea in Britain typically consists of tea, scones, clotted cream, jam, and finger sandwiches, among other items. However, as with any cuisine, there may be variations and regional differences in what is served, so it is possible that deviled eggs could be served at some British tea times.

Teatime Recipes

RECIPE	Sheet Pan Petit Fours		
YIELD	40 Petit Fours	COOKTIME	50 mins.

INGREDIENTS

Nonstick baking spray, for the baking sheet
4 large eggs, cold
1 cup sugar
1 tsp baking powder
1 tsp kosher salt
1 stick (1/2 cup) unsalted butter, melted and cooled to room temp.
1 Tb pure vanilla extract
1 ½ cups all-purpose flour, sifted

Ganache:
10 oz. white chocolate, finely chopped
½ cup heavy cream
Gel food color, in desired color
Sprinkles, in desired color

DIRECTIONS

For the cake: Position an oven rack in the center of the oven and preheat to 375 degrees F. Lightly coat an 18x13-inch sheet pan with nonstick baking spray. Line the bottom with parchment. Set aside.
Beat the eggs, sugar, baking powder and salt in a stand mixer fitted with a whisk attachment on high speed until the mixture is pale and very thick (enough to hold away from the whisk), about 10 mins. Reduce the speed to medium-high and drizzle in the butter and vanilla until just combined, about 10 seconds. Reduce the speed to low and add the sifted flour at once. Beat until just combined, about 5 seconds. Gently fold the batter once or twice using a rubber spatula, then scrape it into the prepared sheet pan. Spread it evenly using the spatula, using broad, gently strokes to keep the batter airy.
Bake, rotating the pan hallway through, until the top is lightly golden, 15 to 18 mins. Cool in the sheet pan for 10 mins, then invert onto a wire rack and cool completely. Punch out about 80 mini cakes using a 1 ½-inch diameter round cookie cutter.

Ganache:
Bring the cream to a simper in a small saucepan over medium heat. Place the white chocolate in the bowl of a stand mixer and pour the hot cream over it. Stir until the chocolate is melted and smooth using a heatproof rubber spatula. Mix in enough food coloring until the desired color is achieved. Place the bowl in the refrigerator until cooled. Return to the stand mixer with the whisk and whip on medium-high speed until light and fluffy. Either pipe or spoon 1 heaping tsp of ganache onto half of the cake rounds. Top each with the remaining cake rounds. Pipe the top of each cake with 1 heaping tsp. of ganache, then top with a pinch of sprinkles.
Serve immediately or store in an airtight container up to 1 day.

THE HISTORY OF SHEET PAN PETIT FOURS:

Petit fours, the delicate and dainty French pastries, have become a beloved part of British teatime traditions. These miniature cakes, cookies, and confections are perfect for indulging in something sweet with your afternoon tea. The history of petit fours can be traced back to the 18th century in France, where they were served as an elegant dessert at royal banquets. Originally, petit fours were made from leftover cake scraps, cut into small squares, glazed, and decorated with icing or marzipan. As French culture and cuisine spread across Europe, petit fours quickly became a popular dessert item in Britain, particularly for special occasions and teatime. Today, petit fours come in various flavors and designs, from delicate almond macarons to decadent chocolate truffles. Whether you prefer a fruity raspberry tartlet or classic vanilla sponge, petit fours offer a delectable and visually stunning addition to any teatime spread. And their bite-sized portions are the perfect way to indulge in a little treat without overindulging. So why not add petit fours to your next teatime gathering and experience some French elegance? Petit fours have become a beloved part of British teatime traditions due to their rich history and exquisite taste. Created in France to use leftover cake scraps, petit fours quickly spread across Europe and became a popular dessert item in Britain. Today, petit fours come in various flavors and designs, thus making them the perfect addition to any teatime spread. In addition, their sheer size and elegant presentation offer a visually stunning and indulgent treat that is perfect for special occasions or simply indulging in something sweet. So, the next time you sit down for a cup of tea, why not add petit fours to your spread and experience French elegance and British tradition?

Teatime Recipes

RECIPE	Classic Cheese Scones		
YIELD	5-6	COOKTIME	20 mins.

INGREDIENTS

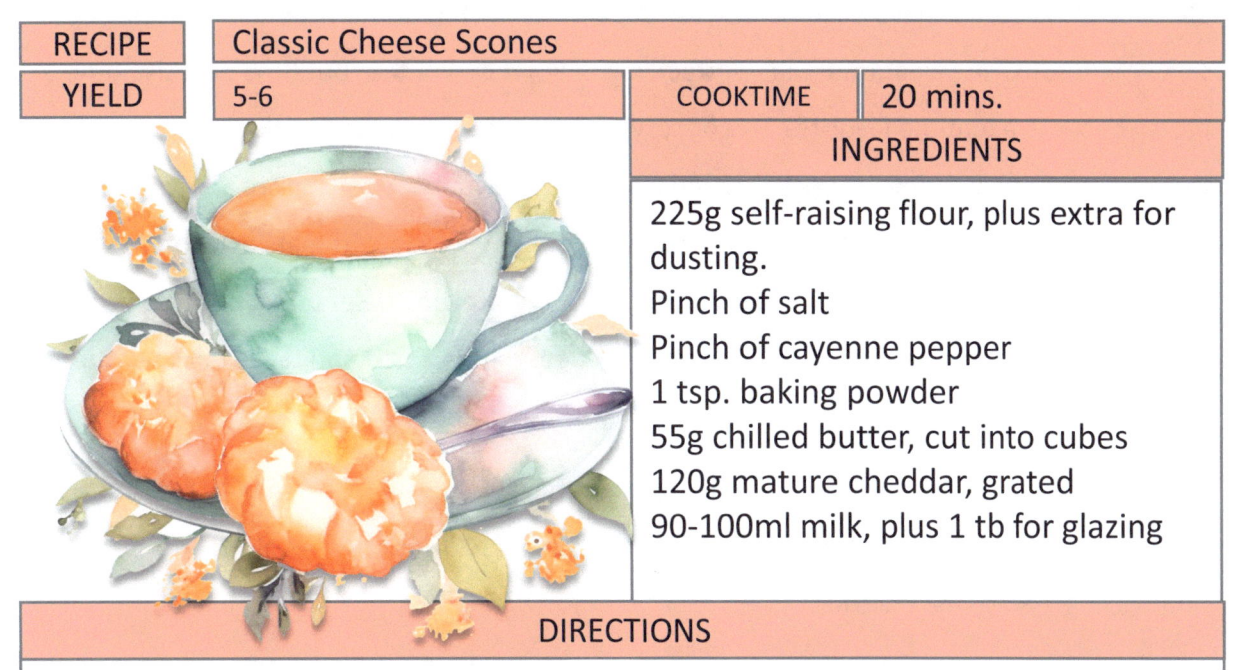

225g self-raising flour, plus extra for dusting.
Pinch of salt
Pinch of cayenne pepper
1 tsp. baking powder
55g chilled butter, cut into cubes
120g mature cheddar, grated
90-100ml milk, plus 1 tb for glazing

DIRECTIONS

1. Heat the oven to 200C/180C fan/gas 6 with a large baking tray inside. Sift the flour, salt, cayenne pepper and baking powder into a bowl, then sift again to make sure the ingredients are thoroughly combined.
2. Add the butter to the bowl and combine with your fingertips to make breadcrumbs. Sprinkle 100g of the cheese into the breadcrumb mixture and rub together until evenly distributed. Try not to mix too much as the heat from your hands may start to melt the butter.
3. Make a well in the center of the mixture and pour in enough milk to give a fairly soft but firm dough. Do not pour in all the milk at once as you may not need it all to get the right consistency.
4. Lightly flour a surface and roll out the dough to approximately 2cm thick. Cut out the scones with a medium (about 8cm) cutter, then put on a sheet of baking parchment, glaze with a little milk and sprinkle with the remaining cheese. Slide onto the hot oven tray.
5. Bake in the oven for 15-20 mins or until golden brown and cooked through.

THE HISTORY OF THE CLASSIC CHEESE SCONES:

Classic cheese scones have become a beloved part of British teatime traditions, offering a savory and satisfying treat that pairs perfectly with a hot cup of tea. But how did this humble pastry become a teatime favorite? The history of scones can be traced back to Scotland in the early 1500s. Over time, scones evolved into the more familiar version we know today, made with flour, butter, and milk or cream instead of being made with oats and cooked on a grill. Classic cheese scones are a variation of this traditional recipe, featuring a savory twist with the addition of grated cheddar cheese. The cheese adds a rich and tangy flavor to the scones, making them a perfect addition to any teatime spread.

Today, cheese scones are a popular choice for teatime, served warm with a dollop of butter or cream cheese. They can also be a delicious alternative to sweet scones alongside sandwiches, cakes, and pastries.

Whether you prefer your scones sweet or savory, there's no denying the deliciousness of a classic cheese scone. So why add some to your next teatime spread and experience British tradition?

Two Sisters Having Tea

Teatime Recipes

RECIPE	
YIELD	COOKTIME

INGREDIENTS

DIRECTIONS

NOTES

Teatime Recipes

RECIPE

YIELD

COOKTIME

INGREDIENTS

DIRECTIONS

NOTES

Teatime Recipes

RECIPE

YIELD

COOKTIME

INGREDIENTS

DIRECTIONS

NOTES

Teatime Recipes

RECIPE	
YIELD	COOKTIME

INGREDIENTS

DIRECTIONS

NOTES

Teatime Recipes

RECIPE	
YIELD	COOKTIME

INGREDIENTS

DIRECTIONS

NOTES

Teatime Recipes

RECIPE	
YIELD		COOKTIME	

INGREDIENTS

DIRECTIONS

NOTES

Teatime Recipes

RECIPE	
YIELD	COOKTIME

INGREDIENTS

DIRECTIONS

NOTES

Teatime Recipes

RECIPE

YIELD

COOKTIME

INGREDIENTS

DIRECTIONS

NOTES

Teatime Recipes

RECIPE	
YIELD	COOKTIME

INGREDIENTS

DIRECTIONS

NOTES

Teatime Recipes

RECIPE	
YIELD	COOKTIME

INGREDIENTS

DIRECTIONS

NOTES

Teatime Recipes

RECIPE	
YIELD		COOKTIME	

INGREDIENTS

DIRECTIONS

NOTES

Teatime Recipes

RECIPE

YIELD

COOKTIME

INGREDIENTS

DIRECTIONS

NOTES

Teatime Recipes

RECIPE

YIELD

COOKTIME

INGREDIENTS

DIRECTIONS

NOTES

Teatime Recipes

RECIPE

YIELD

COOKTIME

INGREDIENTS

DIRECTIONS

NOTES

William Lucas

Lady Caroline

Teapot

Lord Henry Davenport